11/17/95

Christine —

Now if Tom Cruise ever does show up at the Casino you will be prepared. You can have your "fantasy man" autograph the book, and then who knows what...

Of course we all know that this truly is a fantasy as I am more his type than you are, but <u>DREAM ON</u>!

Jerry

TOM CRUISE

TOM CRUISE

Marie Cahill

SMITHMARK

This edition published in 1993 by SMITHMARK Publishers Inc., 16 East 32nd Street, New York, New York 10016.

SMITHMARK books are available for bulk purchase for sales promotion and premium use. For details write or telephone the Manager of Special Sales, SMITHMARK Publishers Inc., 16 East 32nd Street, New York, NY 10016. (212) 532-6600.

Produced by Brompton Books Corp., 15 Sherwood Place, Greenwich, CT 06830.

ISBN 0-8317-8669-8

Printed in Hong Kong

10 9 8 7 6 5 4 3 2 1

Designed by Ruth DeJauregui

Page 1: Tom Cruise is one of Hollywood's major stars.

Page 2: Tom Cruise as 'Maverick' in *Top Gun*, the role that made him a star.

Right: That sexy smile has made Tom Cruise a favorite with moviegoers across America.

Far right: Early in his career, Cruise played a greaser in Francis Ford Coppola's adaptation of *The Outsiders*.

Contents

THE EARLY YEARS

Tom Cruise is as famous for his sexy grin as he is for his steely determination—and both helped make him one of Hollywood's hottest stars. Even before he graduated from high school he had lined up a manager to guide his career. When she started sending him out to do her grocery shopping, he fired her and took his career in his own hands. As soon as he graduated he headed for New York, eager and determined to become a star. Cruise gave himself 10 years to make it as an actor. Within only three, he had catapulted to fame in *Risky Business*.

With his boyish charm and good looks, Cruise soon was an established member of Hollywood's Brat Pack. The challenge was then to prove he could rise above the status of teenage heartthrob. By the age of 24, he had left the Pack behind and was a leading box office draw.

Tom Cruise's determination to succeed should come as no surprise, for the spirit of self-reliance had been forged

Left and above: Tom Cruise's earliest roles were just bit parts, but with each successive part he built a name for himself as an intense and dedicated actor.

Right: The starring role in *Risky Business* made Hollywood take a serious look at Tom Cruise.

Above: Taps was Tom Cruise's second movie. Though his role was a small one, his performance as a psychopathic cadet left a lasting impression.

Left: After Taps, Cruise moved on to Losin' It, playing the part of teenager with an overactive libido. His costar for this embarrassment was Shelly Long.

Right: The youthful cast of Francis Ford Coppola's The Outsiders. Tom Cruise is on the far right.

at an early age. His childhood years were, by his own account, 'very difficult, very pressured.' His family led a nomadic existence, moving from Cruise's birthplace in Syracuse, New York to Canada, to Louisville, Kentucky to wherever his father's job as an electrical engineer took the family. Then, at the age of 12 Cruise found himself cast in the leading role as 'the man of the family' when his parents were divorced. He developed a strong sense of family loyalty to his mother and three sisters that persists to this day.

Cruise, who was born Thomas Cruise Mapother IV on 3 July 1962, was always the new kid at school. Schoolwork, already made difficult by the curriculum differences between schools, was aggravated by dyslexia. To compensate, he excelled at sports.

When he was in high school, Cruise played the part of Nathan Detroit in *Guys and Dolls*. From that moment on, he knew he wanted to be an actor. 'All of a sudden you are up there, and you're doing something you really enjoy, and you are getting all this attention, and people who never turned their heads or said anything before are now saying, "Gee, look at him." And I said to myself, "This is it."'

Five months into his quest for stardom, Cruise landed a bit part in *Endless Love* (1981), a melodramatic teenage love story with Brooke Shields and Martin Hewitt as the

teenage lovers. When the two teenagers become too serious, Brook Shields' parents forbid her from seeing Hewitt. In an attempt to win their approval, Hewitt decides to burn down the house so that he can stage a dramatic rescue. Cruise played the part of the friend who suggested the fire.

Cruise's performance took only a day's work but it brought him enough notice to earn a small part in *Taps* (1981), a film about students who take over a military academy when developers purchase the site. Originally cast in a tiny part—the friend of hotheaded cadet David Shawn—Cruise was moved into the role of Shawn when the actor playing Shawn wasn't making the grade. Director Harold Becker was impressed with Cruise's intensity, but Cruise himself was hesitant. A genuinely nice guy, he was reluctant to take a part from a fellow actor.

Though *Taps* was a well-intentioned allegory on militarism, some critics found its purpose generally muddled and the action predictable. Cruise, however, received favorable reviews as the fanatical military cadet. The part was small, but Cruise masterfully crafted a vivid image of a zealot willing to die for his cause.

Fearful of being typecast as a fanatic, Cruise next opted for a part in *Losin' It* (1983), costarring Shelley Long of *Cheers* fame. In theory, the idea of finding a role as far

removed as possible from David Shawn in *Taps* was a sound one, but in practice his choice of a film was dismal. *Losin' It* was a forgettable teenage exploitation film about a group of friends who head to Tijuana to lose their virginity. It was a blemish on an otherwise flawless career, but Cruise learned a valuable lesson: 'I realized that if you want to grow as an actor, you have to work with the best people. Then you'll be able to have more control over what you do.'

Above: Cruise (right) with Rob Lowe in *The Outsiders*.

Right: Cruise as a greaser in *The Outsiders*. Though his actual onscreen time was relatively limited, Cruise was already earning notice through the Hollywood grapevine.

Left: Clowning around with fellow Brat Packer, Rob Lowe. Hollywood was entering the era of the youth-oriented picture dominated by a group of actors dubbed the Brat Pack. For some, fame faded as quickly as it had arrived. Cruise, however, was soon to break away from the Pack.

Right: To get into the part of Steve, a greaser, Cruise reportedly skimped on showers and had a cap removed from a tooth.

For his next film, *The Outsiders* (1983), Cruise did indeed work with one of the best: Francis Ford Coppola, director of *The Godfather* epic. *The Outsiders* was an adaptation of SE Hinton's novel and is remarkably faithful to the book, which was written when the author was just 15. A story of misunderstood youth set in Tulsa, Oklahoma in the mid-1960s, the plot is reminiscent of *West Side Story* without the music as it relays the conflict between the greasers and the socs (pronounced soshes), the rich kids on the other side of town.

Cruise played a greaser and reportedly got into the role by giving up bathing and removing a cap from a tooth. The film also starred C Thomas Howell as Ponyboy, Ralph Macchio as Johnny and Diane Lane as Cherry Valance.

The Outsiders was especially notable for its cast, which also included Matt Dillon, Emilio Estavez and Rob Lowe who, along with Cruise, Sean Penn, Timothy Hutton, Judd Nelson and a few others, were dubbed the Brat Pack. The term Brat Pack was first coined by David Blum in *New York* magazine to describe the group of rising young male stars with box office magnetism. (Women were later admitted to the ranks of the Brat Pack.) *Taps* was one of the first Brat Pack films, followed by *Tex*, *The Outsiders*, *Wargames*, *The Breakfast Club* and *St Elmo's Fire*, among others.

A cleancut version of the 1960s Rat Pack (Dean Martin, Sammy Davis Jr, Frank Sinatra and Peter Lawford), these young actors, for the most part, went straight from high school to the silver screen, proving that movies about troubled teens and young adults could attract a huge following. The era of the youth-oriented film had begun in earnest. Never before had Hollywood bestowed so much clout on young actors. The members of the Brat Pack were destined to become the hottest thing in Hollywood, but it was Cruise who was the first to break away from the pack and claim the title of star. The film that made that possible was *Risky Business*.

RISKY BUSINESS

Tom Cruise's first major role was the capitalistic teenager in *Risky Business* (1983). In this film, Cruise's character, Joel Goodsen, drives his father's Porsche into Lake Michigan and turns his home into a brothel while his parents are out of town, and in spite of it all, by the film's conclusion, he manages to get accepted into Princeton. Famous for the scene in which Cruise dances in his underwear while playing air guitar to Bob Seger's 'Old Time Rock & Roll,' *Risky Business* was a fun film that audiences enjoyed because Cruise reminded them of their younger brother, a boyfriend, the kid next door, or maybe even themselves. He was the all-American boy, wholesome but not boring, a decent sort just devilish enough to make life interesting.

Director Paul Brickman reportedly was reluctant for Cruise to audition for the part of Joel, concerned that audiences would associate Cruise with the character he

Above and right: Tom Cruise and his costar in *Risky Business*, Rebecca De Mornay. Several months after the film was completed, the two unexpectedly ran into each other and a romance blossomed.

Left: After driving his father's Porsche into Lake Michigan, Joel (Tom Cruise) realizes he has a serious problem on his hands.

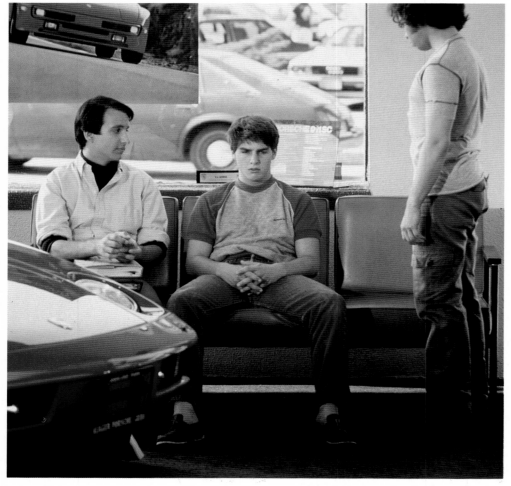

Left: Ray-Bans had an unexpected boost in sales after Tom donned a pair for *Risky Business*.

Right: An engaging smile and a fierce determination are two essential elements in Tom Cruise's formula for success.

Below: Tom Cruise and Rebecca De Mornay pose for a publicity still for *Risky Business*.

played in *Taps*. But once he had the part, the chemistry between actor and director worked like magic.

Chemistry was also at work between Cruise and his costar, Rebecca De Mornay. On screen, he fulfilled every red-blooded teenage boy's sexual fantasy with his love affair with the attractive and business minded call girl.

Off screen, a romance blossomed between the two stars after the film was completed. The couple was a steady item for two years. Cruise is intensely private about his personal life and is reluctant to discuss his relationships with the press. (Over the years Cruise has remained close-mouthed about his personal relationships. In 1987, he married actress Mimi Rogers. When the marriage crumbled three years later, Cruise denied rumors of marital strife until the divorce papers were filed.)

Risky Business was a box office success, grossing $65 million in the theaters. The film gave Cruise the leverage to demand script approval and a million dollar salary. A decade earlier this was unheard of, even among established leading men. What is also noteworthy is the type of character with which Cruise would come to be identified. In contrast to the rebellious youth as portrayed by Marlon Brando and James Dean a generation earlier, the hero for the 1980s was the wholesome, all-American boy. Angst had been replaced with earnestness; self-doubt with self-confidence.

ALL THE RIGHT MOVES

After *Risky Business*, Cruise's next move was playing the football hero in *All the Right Moves* (1983). Set in a Pennsylvania steel town, *All the Right Moves* is a coming of age tale, a sort of working class *Risky Business*. Cruise plays an earnest football player who sees a football scholarship as his ticket out of town. A conflict with his coach (Craig T Nelson) nearly ruins his chance, but in the end their differences are resolved and decency prevails.

At this point, Cruise's career was poised to take off. He instead fell into *Legend* (1985), Ridley Scott's fantasy epic in which he played the peasant Jack, a symbol of innocence and goodness. Cruise was eager to work with Ridley Scott, whose previous credits include *Alien* and *Blade Runner*, but filming was beset with production difficulties (Cruise sprained an ankle; a fire destroyed a set, and in the final product Cruise appears stranded in a sea

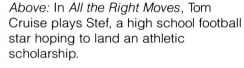

Above: In *All the Right Moves*, Tom Cruise plays Stef, a high school football star hoping to land an athletic scholarship.

Left: Tom Cruise with costar Lea Thompson, who plays his girlfriend. Early in his career Cruise established a reputation for professionalism. Thompson noted that Tom took an interest in her role, working with the director to develop her part.

Right: Tom's next film was Ridley Scott's *Legend*, a fairy tale for grownups.

of special effects. Cruise himself describes his character as 'a color in a Ridley Scott vision.'

Even before filming began, Cruise toyed with the idea of not doing it, but he felt compelled to go through with it. Although he was disappointed with the film, Cruise maintains a positive attitude about it: 'You take what you learn and move on. That's the important thing: to move forward and be better.' His next film was decidedly a forward and better move.

At top: The football heroes—Tom Cruise and costar Christopher Penn.

Above: The Ampipe football team battle the weather and the opposing team on the road to victory.

Right: An athlete himself, Cruise enjoys playing physical roles.

Left and below: Tom Cruise as Jack O'The Green, the legendary hermit of the woods who becomes a hero when he combats the Lord of Darkness and frees the world from its icy curse. The film was filled with marvelous special effects, but the characters lacked development, and Cruise was dissatisfied with his performance.

Right: Jack (Tom Cruise) takes his beloved, played by Mia Sara, on a quest to see the last surviving unicorns.

TOP GUN

The success of *Risky Business* made Tom Cruise a hot property in Hollywood, but *Legend* had made him cautious, so he chose his next part carefully, demanding script approval. Cruise's judgment was right on the mark: *Top Gun* was the number one box office hit of 1986, earning $171.6 million.

The idea for *Top Gun* was born when producers Don Simpson and Jerry Bruckheimer read an article in *California* magazine about the Navy's Fighter Weapons School at Miramar Naval Air Station in San Diego. The Fighter Weapons School, colloquially known as Top Gun, was established in 1969 when it became apparent that pilots had become too dependent on their instruments and didn't know the fundamentals of air-to-air combat. In short, they had lost their dogfighting skills.

Simpson and Bruckheimer, the team behind the hugely successful *Flashdance* and *Beverly Hills Cop*, recognized a hot idea when they saw one. The story of the Top Gun pilots had all the elements of an exhilarating movie. Larger than life, they are the best of the best—the top one percent of all Navy pilots. Passionate and intense, these men are a breed apart. When Simpson and Bruckheimer visited Miramar—aka Fightertown—they took one look at the pilots as they strode to their jets and thought 'Those guys look like Tom Cruise.'

Tom Cruise, however, hesitated when he was offered the

Left: Tom Cruise rocketed to fame in *Top Gun* and joined the ranks of celebrities who are instantly recognized wherever they go.

Right: The sizzling combination of Tom Cruise and Kelly McGillis made *Top Gun* the hottest movie of 1986.

Left: *Top Gun* is based on the exploits of the pilots of the Navy's elite Fighter Weapons School.

Below: Behind the scenes during the making of *Top Gun*.

Right: An extremely intense individual, Cruise is totally focused on his part. For his performance in *Top Gun*, he worked on the script, flew in a jet and earned the respect of the fighter pilots—who initially doubted Cruise's ability to portray one of their own.

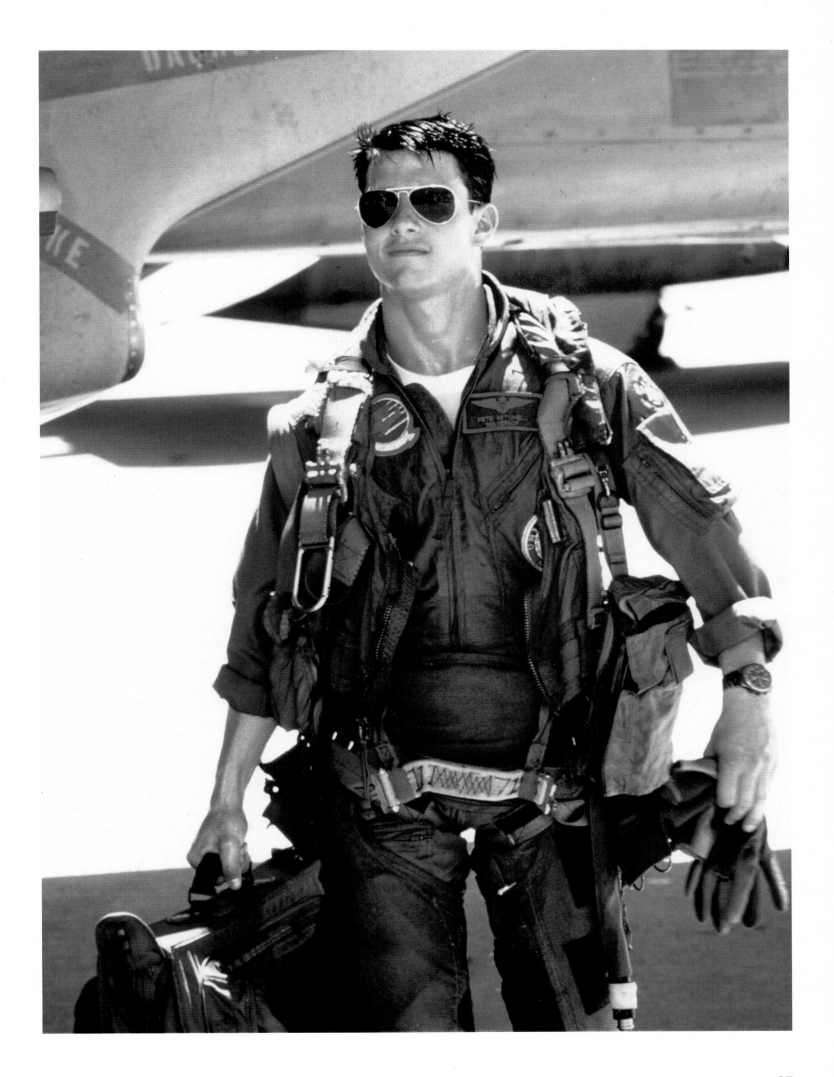

part of Pete 'Maverick' Mitchell in *Top Gun*. He was intrigued by the idea but dissatisfied with the script and demanded having a hand in developing the project before he would consent to doing the film. Producers Don Simpson and Jerry Bruckheimer took his demands in stride because for them Cruise *was* Maverick They never even considered anyone else for the part.

Maverick, Cruise's character, is a brilliant pilot but he doesn't play by the rules. He's an iconoclast, but he's in a position that requires he be a team player. During his training, he is constantly going off on his own, performing death-defying feats, but in a real-life situation his recklessness could mean death for a fellow pilot.

To add complexity to his character, Maverick is haunted by the death of his father, a pilot who was killed in action in Vietnam. The true story behind Duke Mitchell's death is classified information but everyone assumes that he was at fault. Maverick is therefore compelled to prove himself to make up for his father.

In the race to be the best, Maverick is challenged by only one other—Iceman. A foil to Maverick's character, Iceman is the quintessential Navy fighter pilot—brave but level headed, a study of grace under pressure. The Top Gun trophy could easily go to either man. As graduation approaches, Maverick's plane crashes into the sea during a training exercise, killing his partner, Goose (Anthony Edwards). Blaming himself and suffering from a loss of confidence, Maverick is on the verge of abandoning flying forever.

In what will become a recurring theme in many of Cruise's films, we see the hero in a personal struggle, one that requires that he question who he is and what he stands for.

Love interest Charlotte 'Charlie' Blackwood (Kelly McGillis), a civilian Top Gun instructor, helps him to realize that being the best means making mistakes and learning to go on. Maverick seeks advice as well from his flight instructor, Viper (Tom Skerritt). In addition to being the *best* pilot there is, Viper knew Mavericks' father and flew with him on the day he died.

In the ultimate confrontation—an aerial battle with Soviet MiGs—Maverick hesitates but proves his mettle. Still reckless, he has learned that survival means being a team player.

30

Left: After *Top Gun*, Hollywood honored Tom Cruise with a star on Hollywood Boulevard. The ceremony took place on 16 October 1986.

Right: Top Gun had all the ingredients for success—an exhilarating love story, lots of action and a charismatic star.

Top Gun gave audiences a roller coaster ride across the sky—and they loved it. Despite the movie's considerable success, *Top Gun* had its share of detractors who felt that the movie was jingoistic and charged with right wing political propaganda. Cruise and *Top Gun*'s producers were adamant in declaring that the film has nothing to do with war. 'This is not about the F-14,' Cruise explains, 'it's a film about the men who fly the F-14. These guys get up there and it's terrifying. They're not sitting in their seats hoping for a war. They love to fly. This film's about relationships, about independence, about understanding—about excellence.' Don Simpson echoed those sentiments with his description of *Top Gun*: '*Top Gun* is definitely about nobility, incredible nobility, dedication to excellence.'

The plot of *Top Gun* did focus on the pursuit of excellence and it did have an electrifying love story, but the planes were the gimmick that helped make the film work. In fact, it was a ride in an A-4 with the Blue Angels aerial demonstration team that persuaded Cruise to make the film.

The Navy brass supported the film, seeing it as an opportunity to boost recruitment. After the film *An Officer and a Gentleman* was released, recruiting levels increased dramatically. The Navy had not cooperated with that film in any way, but they were prepared to make the most of their association with *Top Gun*, and even set up recruiting booths outside theaters where the movie was playing.

The Navy pilots, however, were another story. Cruise had to win the approval of the pilots, who initially were skeptical that he could portray one of their own—a man who lived life on the edge. Cruise is an actor known for his intensity and soon proved that he had the right stuff. He did his own stunts for the rescue at sea sequence and, on a more personal level, he took part in 'Animal Night,' a notorious weekly event of heavy drinking and partying.

After *Top Gun*, Tom Cruise was instantly recognizable wherever he went. On his way to becoming a Movie Star with a capital M, his next picture would give him the opportunity to work with the best and move him one step closer to joining their ranks.

THE COLOR OF MONEY

op Gun made Tom Cruise a major box office draw at the age of only 24. The movie was such a roaring success that Cruise could easily have made a sequel at an exorbitant fee. Instead, he wanted to try other kinds of roles so that he could grow as an actor. In a young actor's dream come true, Cruise was given the opportunity to star opposite one of Hollywood's most enduring icons—Paul Newman—in Martin Scorsese's *The Color of Money* (1986).

The Color of Money continues the story of Fast Eddie Felson (Paul Newman), last seen in 1961 in Robert Rossen's *The Hustler*. Although technically a sequel, the film does not conform to the usual definition of a Hollywood sequel. Sequels, which often fail to live up to the standard of the original, are typically released as soon as possible to capitalize on the success of the first film. In the case of *The Color of Money*, a generation had gone by and moviegoers' curiosity about the fate of Eddie Felson had long since past. Indeed, many of the present day moviegoers weren't even born when *The Hustler* was released. Sequels also tend to feature the same cast and crew, but with the exception of Newman, the people involved in *The Color of Money* were completely different.

The Color of Money is set 25 years after *The Hustler*. Eddie, now a slick liquor salesman, is still a hustler, but of

Left: Paul Newman and Tom Cruise in *The Color of Money*.

Above: Newman as 'Fast Eddie,' gets tough with his young protégé.

Right: The pairing of one of Hollywood's hottest young stars with one of its icons was a brilliant move by director Martin Scorsese.

Left, above: As Fast Eddie Felson (whom we first saw 25 years earlier in *The Hustler*), Paul Newman sees money-making potential in Vincent (Tom Cruise). He persuades Vincent and his girlfriend to go on the road with him, touring the pool halls of the Midwest in preparation for a big tournament.

Left, below: A tense moment between Vincent and his girlfriend, Carmen (Mary Elizabeth Mastrantonio).

Right: Tom Cruise as Vincent Lauria, a gifted young pool player.

another sort. He has become everything he despised. When he meets Vincent Lauria (Tom Cruise), a young, talented pool player, he is reminded of himself long ago. Vincent is totally guileless; he plays pool for the joy of playing—and winning. Vincent could use his skills to make a lot of money, but he is unschooled in the art of hustling. Eddie Felson, however, sees a golden opportunity and forms a partnership with Vincent and his girlfriend, Carmen, (Mary Elizabeth Mastrantonio). Eddie will teach him what he knows, manage everything and take 60 percent of Vincent's winnings. The three of them set out for the pool rooms of the Midwest, with Atlantic City and a nine-ball tournament their ultimate destination.

To educate Vincent, Eddie must corrupt him. From Eddie's perspective, Vincent is a problem student. He is, in the words of his girlfriend, a sweet kid, and in one of his first pool room hustles, he refuses to take money from an old man. Typically, however, he is so caught up in the joy of playing that he refuses to 'dump' a game to sucker an opponent and thus blows the chance to win big later on.

As for Eddie, the love of pool has been rekindled and he ends up being hustled himself. Angry and frustrated with himself, Eddie says there is nothing more he can teach Vincent. The two part company, each bound for Atlantic City, where they end up squaring off at the pool table. Having seduced Vincent with his creed that 'money won is twice as sweet as money earned,' Eddie discovers that Vincent has learned his lessons well, but in exchange for riches Vincent has sacrificed his innocence and integrity. Vincent's fall from grace notwithstanding, *The Color of Money* is a redemption story, for in corrupting Vincent, Eddie has found his own salvation.

Ostensibly based on the novel by Walter Tevis, who also wrote *The Hustler*, all the story has in common with Tevis' novel is the title. Martin Scorsese, director of such critically acclaimed films as *Taxi Driver* and *Raging Bull*, asked novelist Richard Price (*The Wanderers*, *Bloodbrothers* and *The Breaks*) to do the screenplay from scratch, with Scorsese and Newman joining him in the revision process. With the screenplay in good shape, Scorsese and Newman turned their sights to finding the right actor to play the part of Vincent. They never considered anyone else for the part, though they had dozens of young actors to choose from, given Hollywood's recent emphasis on youth-oriented movies.

Top Gun proved that Cruise was boffo at the box office. While Cruise's previous films were entertaining and commercially successful, they were the kinds of films that critics would deride as lacking artistic value. Not so *The Color of Money*. A well-crafted film, it captures the sleazy and intense atmosphere of the poolrooms that pepper the cites of the Rust Belt. All the elements, from cinematography to dialogue, work together to form something greater than the sum total of its parts. The cast was no less than superb. The durable Newman, who 30 years ago excited audiences with his portrayal of the sexy, brooding antihero in *The Long Hot Summer*, *Cat on a Hot Tin Roof* and *Hud*, and has been wowing them ever since, won a long-

deserved Academy Award for his razor sharp performance as Eddie. Newcomer Mary Elizabeth Mastrantonio was superb as Vincent's hard, ambitious girlfriend, and Helen Shaver gave a bitingly realistic portrayal of Newman's oft-disappointed, but loyal, lover.

As for Tom Cruise, the role of Vincent Lauria elevated him from his teen hero image to serious young actor. Full of raw, kinetic energy, Cruise plays Vincent as a rock and roll pool star, twirling his cue stick at an unseen opponent. Playing pool to Warren Zevon's 'Werewolves of London,' he is athletic and manic—and all the shots but one were done by Cruise himself. He worked with his trainer, Mike Sigel, for months and spent countless sleepless nights playing pool before filming started in Chicago.

While the film was an undeniable boost to Cruise's career, the teaming of a Hollywood legend with one of the silver screen's hottest young stars gave *The Color of Money* major box office potential. Jeffrey Katzenberg, production chief at Disney Studios (the film was released by Touchstone Pictures, Disney's 'grown-up' film arm) said the addition of Cruise to the cast gave the film top priority, expanding the audience appeal of a film that already had 'great artistic integrity.'

Both Scorsese and Newman had high praise for Cruise. Like Simpson and Bruckheimer, the producers of *Top Gun*, they were impressed by Cruise's commitment to excellence and determination to succeed. Whatever the project, Cruise is totally focused on what he is doing, approaching each role with a perfectionist's eye.

Although Cruise was only 24 when *The Color of Money* was made, he had already formed his own production company to develop projects for himself. Like his costar Paul Newman, he always has his eyes open for good roles to play.

Left: Cruise will one day join Newman in the pantheon of stars.

Above: Tom Cruise with his former wife, actress Mimi Rogers.

COCKTAIL

As could easily have happened with a young man who suddenly struck it rich, Tom Cruise didn't let success go to his head. He remained a pleasant, down-to-earth, likable guy. Behind the scenes, Cruise is known for his politeness and earnest attitude about his career. His philosophy is to always work with the best. After *The Color of Money*, he was offered the chance to work with director Roger Donaldson in *Cocktail*. Donaldson was riding high on the success of *No Way Out*, an edge-of-your-seat drama, and Cruise's role in *Cocktail* promised to be a gripping study of a character's personal development.

A parable of the 1980s, *Cocktail* (1988) focuses on the fast-paced, fast track singles' world. Tom Cruise plays Brian Flanagan, a fresh faced young man just out of the Army in search of his version of the American dream. To use Cruise's description, 'Brian is a wanna-be, a guy who wants to be a yuppie.' Brian leaves his home in Queens and heads for New York, determined to strike it rich on Wall Street. After repeated job rejections, he puts his career goals on hold and takes a job as a bartender. There, he meets Doug Coughlin (Bryan Brown), a seasoned pro on life's fast track. Coughlin convinces Brian that the ticket to

These pages: In *Cocktail*, Cruise played Brian Flanagan, an ambitious young man who becomes one of New York's 'star' bartenders.

success can be found behind a bar, where they have easy access to New York's rich and famous. The pair become star bartenders, the toast of Manhattan's hip Upper East Side—and Brian is seduced by this seemingly glamorous lifestyle.

After a falling out with Coughlin, Brian moves to Jamaica, where he hopes to earn enough money to finance his own bar in New York. In the meantime, he falls in love with an artist, Jordan Mooney (Elizabeth Shue). Despite his attraction to Jordan, Brian still lusts for money and life in the fast track. He becomes involved with a successful businesswoman, with the goal of becoming a sales manager in her company. Brian, however, has not sunk so low that he totally abandons his personal ethics. When he sees what he has become, he ends the relation-

ship and goes in search of Jordan and the meaning of life.

Meanwhile, Coughlin has discovered that the glamorous lifestyle is empty and, in despair, he slashes his own throat. In his grief over his friend's death, Brian discovers that true love is worth more than all the money on Wall Street. He rejects his self-centered lifestyle and mends his tattered relationship with Jordan.

Cruise described *Cocktail* as 'a stern, serious depiction of what the American dream is now. And the character never really becomes this great success. In the end, what the film says is "You have to be happy with where you are and who you are." '

Unfortunately, the film never lived up to that basic premise. It could have been a compelling commentary on the value modern society places on material wealth. Instead,

Left: While bartending in Jamaica, Brian meets Jordan Mooney, a down-to-earth artist.

Above: The young lovers relax in Jamaica.

Right: Back in New York, Brian attempts to renew his relationship with Jordan.

Left: To add flair to the part of Brian Flanagan, Tom Cruise went to bartending school.

Above: Cocktail may have fallen flat, but Cruise's career is flying high.

Cocktail fell flat. It had neither the excitement of *Top Gun* nor the gritty realism of *The Color of Money*. Moreover, the movie was never able to capture the trendy atmosphere of the New York night scene. Although he would prove in his next film that he was capable of playing a self-centered individual, Cruise's portrayal of Brian Flanagan never quite hit the mark.

In spite of negative reviews, the film grossed $175 million—a real testament to Cruise's drawing power—and Cruise moved on to better things, his career untarnished.

RAIN MAN

While filming *Cocktail*, Cruise had a another project in the works, one of the most exciting of his brief career. The role of Charlie Babbitt in *Rain Man* would complete his apprenticeship and persuade the Hollywood community that Tom Cruise had grown up.

Rain Man (1988) is the story of Charlie Babbitt, a slick, self-centered wheeler dealer in gray market cars. When his father dies, leaving $3 million to the autistic brother (Dustin Hoffman) he didn't even know existed, Charlie feels robbed of his inheritance. Intending to somehow seize control of the fortune he has been denied, Charlie impulsively takes his brother Raymond from the institution in Cincinnati, Ohio where he has lived in peaceful isolation for the last 20 years.

Raymond suffers from autism, a crippling personality disorder that makes him unable to function in the real world. The condition is characterized by an inability to form normal human attachments. Incapable of responding to or displaying affection, Raymond is disturbed by the touch of another human being. His existence is ordered by the strict routine of the institution and any deviation from that routine is stressful, even terrifying. Though unable to relate to people in a normal way, Raymond is an autistic savant who possesses an incredible affinity for numbers. For reasons medical science cannot explain, some autistics are capable of incredible mental feats. Raymond, for example, can easily multiply four digit figures in his head, count an entire box of toothpicks as it falls to the floor or memorize the phone book.

In his own way, Charlie Babbitt is as autistic as his brother. Estranged from his father since the age of 16, he too is unable to express his emotions. Concerned only about money, he is unable to reveal his innermost feelings to Italian girlfriend Susanna (Valeria Golino).

What began as a kidnapping becomes a journey of spiritual growth for Charlie Babbitt. He cannot fly back to Los Angeles because Raymond is terrified of flying, nor can he drive on the freeway or in the rain without sending Raymond into a fit. Thus, Charlie is forced to drive the backroads of America with his brother Raymond. Over the course of the journey he learns to cope with his brother's needs and fears and in doing so comes to terms with himself. All his adult life Charlie has gotten by on charm or his ability to con people, neither of which will work with Raymond. Now, he is forced to relate to another human being on that person's terms.

Left: Tom Cruise portrays Charlie Babbitt and Dustin Hoffman plays his autistic brother, Raymond, in *Rain Man*.

Right: Dustin Hoffman's moving performance of an autistic savant garnered him an Academy Award.

Las Vegas is the turning point in Charlie's development. With his company on the verge of financial ruin, Charlie uses Raymond's mathematical ability to win at the tables of Las Vegas. Saved from disaster, Charlie thanks Raymond and apologizes for losing his temper earlier. Up to this point, Charlie has been a callous individual who has never needed anyone nor felt the need to apologize for his actions. Raymond, of course, is unable to understand the emotions that Charlie is expressing and screams in terror when Charlie tries to hug him.

At this point it seems that a happy ending is on its way and that Charlie will be granted custody of his brother. But that is not to be. Autism is not a disease that can be cured; it is a condition that persists. In a bittersweet ending, the two brothers part as Raymond, under the care of his doctor, heads back to the institution in Cincinnati.

Dustin Hoffman's performance as Raymond will likely be remembered as one of the best of his career, but Cruise was the engine that made the film run. Audiences cannot identify with Raymond, but they could watch Charlie, first despising him for being selfish and callous and then be heartened as he matures into a caring individual. Though the film is about the two brothers, it pivots on Charlie's personal growth. The scenes in which the two brothers interact are both poignant and comical.

Rain Man was the movie that almost didn't get made. It took two years, four directors and six screenwriters to finish it. The script underwent major changes, with the part of Raymond shifting from a loveable retarded person to an autistic who is incapable of expressing emotions.

Marty Brest (*Beverly Hills Cop*) was the original director, and during his tenure, Hoffman and Cruise were signed up. Working with Dustin Hoffman was a dream come true for Tom Cruise. Hoffman was Cruise's idol. Along with Sean Penn and Timothy Hutton, he used to sit outside Hoffman's house unable to get up the nerve to knock on the door. Hoffman was equally excited about working with the young actor, recognizing in Cruise a shared intensity about their work. But director Brest quit, causing inevitable delays in filming.

Steven Spielberg then expressed an interest in directing the film. He and Hoffman visited autistic facilities together, but Spielberg was involved in the making of *Indiana Jones and the Last Crusade* and couldn't handle both films. Next, Hoffman called Sydney Pollack about the project. Hoffman and Pollack had worked together on *Tootsie*. Though the end product was a success, filming was marked by battles between director and star. Nonetheless, Pollack was eager to work on the film and brought in new writers and a crew. Then, he too quit.

Finally, Barry Levinson (*The Natural, Tin Men*) came on board. By this time it was a race against the clock to finish the picture in time for the lucrative Christmas season. Where the other directors had worried about the plot,

Left: In a bittersweet ending, Charlie realizes that Raymond cannot cope in the outside world.

Above: The fruits of two years' labor were reaped at the 1988 Academy Award ceremony.

Left: Charlie keeps his guard up with everyone, including his girlfriend, played by Valeria Golino.

Right: Cruise and his wife, Mimi Rogers, were on hand to share in *Rain Man*'s triumph.

Levinson concentrated on the characters, realizing that their relationship would dictate the action. Levinson fine-tuned the script, changing Charlie's savvy lawyer girlfriend to a sweet (but volatile) Italian girl and added the Abbott and Costello routine that Raymond goes through when he is nervous. Levinson even stepped in at the last minute to play the part of the psychiatrist at the custody hearing.

Above all, Levinson recognized that this is a movie that could *not* have a neat, happy resolution. While other directors had tried to create a plot device to keep the two brothers together, Levinson understood that formula would not work.

The trials and tribulations that went into making the film paid off in the end. *Rain Man* won Best Picture for 1988, Hoffman walked away with a well-deserved Academy Award and Cruise earned the respect of the Hollywood community and the chance to play the leading role in a major drama—*Born on the Fourth of July*.

BORN ON THE FOURTH OF JULY

Up to this point in his career, Tom Cruise was regarded by some as just another pretty face. *Born on the Fourth of July* made people take notice and view him as a serious actor.

Born on the Fourth of July (1989) is based on the true story of Ron Kovic, a young man who joins the Marines because he loves his country and wants to stop the Communist menace. He returns from Vietnam a paraplegic and, when confronted with his country's hypocrisy, becomes a leader in the antiwar movement. Cruise plays the part of Kovic, from the age of 17, when he is struggling to win a wrestling title, through his personal battles with being a paraplegic and his public fight against the war, to age 27 and his triumphant appearance at the 1976 Democratic convention.

Director Oliver Stone (*Platoon*) pulled out all the stops for *Born on the Fourth of July*. The opening scenes are rich with symbols of Americana: baseball, the Fourth of July parade, a young boy's first kiss. Ten-year-old Ronnie Kovic is the typical all-American boy, but there is something

Tom Cruise's convincing portrayal of paraplegic Ron Kovic in *Born on the Fourth of July* earned him a nomination for an Academy Award. Cruise's performance spanned 10 years, from Kovic's senior year in high school (*left*) to his appearance (*right*) at the 1976 Democratic Convention.

special—an earnest quality that sets him apart. While watching President Kennedy's inaugural address, his mother tells of the dream she had the night before: Ronnie was making a speech—he was important and could make a difference.

By the time Cruise appears on the screen, as the teenage Ron Kovic, the audience is prepared for somebody special, but it is a specialness born out of the ordinary. Ron is 'everyboy'—decent, hard-working and sincere.

Cruise's performance reveals an amazing depth. As the 17-year-old Kovic, he is innocent, filled with enthusiasm and undying love for his country. His upbringing has taught

him that life calls for struggle and sacrifice. We see this message repeated again and again, from the speeches of the high school coach and the Marine recruiting officer to the religious icons of the Catholic church.

After the war, Cruise effectively portrays the anger and frustrations his character feels as he grapples with his emotions about himself and his country. In gut-wrenching scenes, we see him vent his anger against his mother, his church, his society—everything he has ever believed in. Effectively conveying that emotion to an audience requires that an actor be totally involved in a role.

In addition to being emotionally exhausting, the role was

physically demanding. Cruise did not sit passively in a wheelchair. He was thrown from the chair and dragged across the ground, sparred with another wheelchair vet, got trampled in riots and was involved in various barroom brawls.

Cruise considers the role to be the most important of his career, and also the biggest gamble. The part is indeed the most ambitious of Cruise's career and his performance is totally convincing. Cruise's depiction of life in a wheelchair is infused with authenticity. To prepare for the part, Cruise spent time with paraplegics at a VA hospital. He lived in a wheelchair for days on end and would have taken a serum that induces temporary paralysis had the film's insurers allowed him to do so. This is typical Cruise behavior—for *Top Gun* he went up in a jet, for *The Color of Money* he spent eight weeks learning to shoot pool and for *Cock-*

tail he went to bartending school and tended bar a few nights in a Manhattan hot spot.

Ron Kovic himself was personally involved with the project, and prior to filming had voiced some doubts about Cruise's ability to express the range of emotions that the part called for. After his first meeting with the young actor his doubts were laid to rest. The two men shared a similar background—Catholic, working class, sports.

Above all, Cruise was determined to play the part and agreed to work for scale rather than his usual multimillion dollar fee, even though the film was something of a gamble. A wheelchair-bound vet was a far cry from the other roles he had played. Cruise's good looks and smile are what draw audiences to his films. *Cocktail* demonstrates that a movie doesn't have to be good—all it needs is Tom Cruise. Prior to the release of *Born on the Fourth of July,*

Universal Pictures was reluctant to release stills of Cruise in a wheelchair, concerned that audiences would reject that image of the sexy star.

Born on the Fourth of July made audiences alter their perception of Tom Cruise. Cruise rejects the notion that his characters belong to the same mold, preferring to concentrate on each character's personal motivation. To audiences, however, the similarities are part of the Cruise formula for success. To many, the typical Tom Cruise character is a hard worker and equally hard partier. His characters revel in taking risks. Though they are generally troubled by a personal crisis, they deal with the situation and emerge stronger and better people. Sexy and athletic, they are involved with attractive, intelligent women.

In stark contrast to his previous roles, Cruise in *Born on the Fourth of July* is neither a nice guy nor nice looking. Director Oliver Stone took the typical Cruise persona and turned it upside down. Instead of fun and excitement, we are confronted with the ugly realities of war. We experience the horror that Kovic and his fellow soldiers feel when they realize they have slaughtered a defenseless group of women and children. Only 17 minutes of the action is set in Vietnam, but it is undeniably a film about the war.

Audiences responded enthusiastically to Cruise's performance, which earned him a nomination for an Academy Award. With his gripping portrayal of Ron Kovic, Tom Cruise is now clearly positioned as one of Hollywood's leading stars.

At top: In Mexico, Ron (Tom Cruise) meets fellow veteran and paraplegic (Willem Dafoe).

Above: Tom Cruise and Ron Kovic win the Golden Globe Award.

Right: Tom Cruise is the People's Choice.

DAYS OF THUNDER

Days of Thunder premiered the weekend of the Fourth of July 1990, earning $40 million in its first two weeks. The perfect summer movie, it featured action, drama and romance. Set against the backdrop of the NASCAR (National Association for Stock Car Auto Racing) circuit, Days of Thunder dealt with a subject close to Tom Cruise's own heart. Cruise, in fact, wrote the original outline for the story and shares story credit with screenwriter Robert Towne.

Since teaming with Paul Newman in The Color of Money in 1986, Cruise, like Newman himself, has been an ardent fan of race cars. After experiencing the Daytona 500, the Super Bowl of stock car racing, Cruise had wanted to do a movie about it.

Several movies have been made about racing, but many took the low-brow, comedy route. Tom Cruise wanted to make a movie that captured the excitement and intensity of stock car racing. He wanted the audience to feel what it is like to be at the track—to experience the scream of the engines as the cars whiz by the stands, the smell of burning rubber and the sensation of going 200 mph as a car zooms down the straightaway. He wanted the audience to feel what it is like to be door-to-door, paint-to-paint with modified Luminas and Thunderbirds. In addition, Cruise wanted to give the audience more than just action; he wanted the audience to be involved with the characters. 'I want the racing scenes to punctuate what's happening in the characters' lives,' Cruise explained.

In Days of Thunder, Tom Cruise plays Cole Trickle, an ambitious and daring but inexperienced driver who is discovered by local businessman Tim Daland (Randy Quaid). A rookie driver, Cole is fiercely independent. He does things his way, and as a result burns out his tires instead of winning races. When he learns to trust pit crew chief Harry Hogge (Robert Duvall), he matures professionally as well as personally. Cole is on his way to a winning year until a fiery crash threatens to end his career. Though temporarily blinded, he is soon given a clean bill of health and can return to racing. His own fear, however, works against him and he deliberately blows an engine in midrace rather than finish and risk another injury.

His fears are compounded with the realization that rival driver Rowdy Burns (Michael Rooker) was injured far more seriously than he was. Both men are suffering from denial: Rowdy won't admit he needs to return to the hospital and Cole cannot deal with his fear. Cole's doctor, Claire Lewicki (Nicole Kidman), who is now his lover, forces Cole to re-examine his values. As his doctor, she has had to look deeply into his eyes, and Cole's eyes were indeed the window to his soul. She has seen and understood his doubts. Most of all, she understands that Cole's desire to be in control is at the heart of his problems. This is why

Right: In Days of Thunder, Tom Cruise plays race car driver Cole Trickle.

Left: Cole (Tom Cruise), Tim Daland (Randy Quaid) and Harry Hogge (Robert Duvall) plot a strategy for becoming a winning team.

Cole's accident is all the more disturbing: no one could understand how it happened. The car that hit him came out of nowhere and there was no way Cole could control what was happening. In a pivotal scene, Claire angrily tells Cole that control is an illusion and only 'infantile ego-maniacs don't know that.'

Cruise, incidentally, found love on screen and off with his Australian costar, and he and Kidman were married late in 1990.

Tom Cruise personally objected to Claire's speech and wanted it deleted, declaring that he *can* control things. Screenwriter Robert Towne pointed out that it was crucial to the plot because it was supposed to make Cruise's character react in just the way that Cruise himself had. The speech stayed in. Cole is thus forced to confront his fears. He, in turn, persuades Rowdy to seek medical help. Realizing that he may never race again, Rowdy asks Cole to race his car for him at Daytona. Cole cannot refuse. Hanging in the balance is Rowdy's financial well-being (he will literally lose the family farm) as well as his own self-image.

Still plagued by self-doubt, Cole climbs into the driver's seat and faces the ultimate challenge—the Daytona 500. With Claire and Harry's encouragement, Cole is triumphant and wins NASCAR's most coveted award, the Winston Cup.

Days of Thunder shows the highly technical and professional side of racing, as well as the emotional high that comes from racing. The film reveals both the brutality and exhilaration that is stock car racing. The audience sees drivers looming in the rear view mirror as they viciously strike the car ahead of them. Known as rubbin' in racing parlance, these maneuvers are all part of the daily grind. Some professional drivers, however, have criticized the film, maintaining that *Days of Thunder* is not an accurate picture of stock car racing because it exaggerates the amount of rubbing and bumping that goes on at the track.

Criticisms aside, a great deal of research went into making the movie. The characters and events are based on real life racing anecdotes and people. Screenwriter Robert Towne interviewed drivers, owners, engine builders and sportscasters about the racing life. Legendary driver Richard Petty relayed how he had once suffered from temporary blindness following an accident, thus providing the basis for Cole's medical condition. The part of Tim Daland was inspired by Rick Hendrick, a Charlotte, North Carolina businessman and racing team owner who served as technical advisor for the film. Robert Duvall's Harry Hogge was based on Harry Hyde, a crusty crew chief with a penchant for moonshine. Hyde had been mentor to driver Tim Richmond, a James Dean-type who died in 1989. Richmond had been involved with an opthamologist. Those elements were woven into the character of Cole Trickle.

Filming was done with the permission of NASCAR officials on location at Phoenix, Charlotte and Daytona. Two Paramount cars were actually allowed to compete in the Daytona 500. (They did 40 laps.) To add to the authenticity, Tom Cruise attended the Bob Bondurant School of High Performance Driving and, with the exception of the most difficult stunts, did all his own driving. He even set a record for a non-certified NASCAR driver, doing several laps at 182 mph. Producer Don Simpson accompanied Cruise to racing school and played the bit part of Aldo Benedetti, a rival driver.

Obtaining permission from NASCAR was only the first obstacle to overcome. In addition to the obvious problems

Left: Cruise and his wife, Mimi. Her departure from the set sparked rumors of marital strife. Soon after, the couple divorced. *Above:* Cruise is as intense behind the scenes as he is in front of the camera.

Cole Trickle

Though each role has a distinct persona, certain similarities can be drawn between Cruise's characters. His heroes tend to be naturally talented, although they may suffer from a brief period of self-doubt (*left*). When put to the test they overcome their fears and emerge triumphant (*right*).

inherent in filming dangerous stunts, the filming was marked by weather delays. But perhaps the biggest problem was the script itself. Warren Skaaren, who had been part of the *Top Gun* team, was hired to do the screenplay, but after seven drafts the story still wasn't where he wanted it to be.

Robert Towne took over at this point. Towne had a reputation for fixing scripts under a heated deadline. He salvaged the screenplays for *Bonnie and Clyde* and *The Godfather*, though his work went uncredited, and won an Oscar for writing *Chinatown*. Unable to identify with Skaaren's script, Towne started from scratch, writing nonstop, literally handing the lines over to the actors just before the scene was filmed.

To film one of the race sequences, Towne read the lines to Cruise over his earphones as the scene was being filmed. In the movie, when Cole appears to listening intently to his crew chief, Cruise is actually listening to his next line.

If the theme of *Days of Thunder* is reminiscent of *Top Gun*, Cruise's blockbuster hit of 1986, that is not surprising. The same team that created *Top Gun* was behind *Days of Thunder* produced by Don Simpson and Jerry Bruckheimer and director Tony Scott.

In addition to the personnel, the plots of the two movies share certain key elements. In both films, the main character is a brash young man involved in a high risk profession. *Top Gun*'s Maverick flies fighter jets, while Cole of *Days of*

Thunder drives race cars. Each character undergoes a traumatic event and loses his confidence. Maverick's plane goes down and his best friend dies; Cole crashes and temporarily loses his sight. After much soul searching, the character regains his confidence, with the help of a mentor who is a respected veteran in his field, and a woman who is older, more mature and highly educated. Maverick turns to Viper, his Top Gun instructor and friend of his father, and to Charlie, his civilian instructor. Cole depends on Harry, his pit crew chief, and Claire, his doctor.

Despite the similarities, Cruise insists that *Days of Thunder* is not *Top Gun* on wheels. 'Cole and Maverick are different people going through things differently.' Cruise, in fact, objects to the notion that there is a stereotypical Tom Cruise image—a young, energetic, sexy character—arguing that if you look at the various characters, 'there's a range.' Indeed, Cruise even changes his body to suit the character. Maverick in *Top Gun* was well-toned, while Joel in *Risky Business* was softer, heavier.

Cruise is always on the lookout for new, different kinds of roles, adhering to the philosophy that an actor who doesn't attempt different things grows stale. At one point, he was considering *Rush*, based on Kim Wozencraft's novel about junkie cops, but he was concerned about its depiction of drug use. Cruise had previously turned down the lead in *Bright Lights, Big City* because he felt the film glorified drug use, even though its basic message was antidrug.

BEYOND THE BRAT PACK

Since he first appeared on the show business scene in 1981, Tom Cruise has been attracting attention. His first roles, though small, earned him enough notice to move on to bigger and better parts. With each new part, the media tracked his career relentlessly. In 1984, *People* magazine predicted Tom Cruise would be one of tomorrow's stars. He was among 'The 25 Most Intriguing People of 1986,' and in 1990, *People* declared him 'The Sexiest Man Alive.'

Cruise's most ardent desire is to be regarded as a serious actor, not as a sex symbol. He won't pose for beefcake posters, and he oversees the release of all movie stills so that none emphasize sex over substance. Nonetheless, sex appeal is a big part of Cruise's success. Perhaps Jerry Bruckheimer, who worked with him on *Top Gun* and *Days of Thunder* said it best: 'Guys want to like him and girls want to be with him.'

In spite of stardom, Tom Cruise remains a down-to-earth, likeable guy. He is known for his politeness and words like 'sir' and 'ma'am' pepper his vocabulary. High

Left: In 1983, Tom Cruise found romance onscreen and off with his *Risky Business* costar Rebecca De Mornay.

Right: Tom Cruise escorts his mother to the Academy Awards in 1990.

school seniors across the United States voted him 'Top Hero of Young America' in 1988. Following the release of *Days of Thunder* in 1990, Tom Cruise stayed extremely busy, although he was out of the public eye with no film releases in 1991.

In May 1991, Imagine Films Entertainment began filming on location in Montana and Ireland for the film *Far and Away*. Directed by Ron Howard, *Far and Away* starred Cruise, along with his wife Nicole Kidman in an epic tale of the triumphs and tragedies of Irish immigration to America's plains states.

Far and Away was a powerful and moving picture and it gave Tom and Nicole a chance to work with one another on a major film project. The film was ultimately released to critical acclaim in 1992 and distributed by Universal.

Cruise hardly had a chance to take a breath between the filming for *Far and Away* and his having to begin work on another film in October 1991. This film, called *A Few Good Men*, was destined to be one of 1992's major films. Directed by Rob Reiner, it was shot on location in Washington, DC and in the studio in Los Angeles. Borrowing the advertising slogan of the US Marine Corps for its title, *A Few Good Men* is a chilling courtroom drama involving a Marine Corps court-martial.

The story begins with a barracks murder on a Marine base, and Tom Cruise, playing a US Navy lawyer, is called in as the prosecutor in the court-martial. A Navy lawyer is involved because technically the Marine Corps is a part of the Navy. At first, he views the case as simply routine, but he soon discovers that it goes much deeper—penetrating the heart of the morality of the Military Code of Conduct, a code that demands unquestioned acceptance of authority and unquestioned following of orders.

At top: Cruise with Paul Newman and Mary Elizabeth Mastrantonio in Martin Scorsese's *The Color of Money*.

Right: The young star is awarded a star of his own on Hollywood Boulevard.

Cruise's colleague, played by Demi Moore, urges him to recognize the far-reaching moral and sociological importance of the case and not simply go through the motions. At first, Cruise is reluctant. Like many military officers in non-combat jobs, he sees his military career as simply a stepping stone to a lucrative private practice in civilian life. He wants to not make waves. He wishes to do his job and successfully put the rigidity of military life behind him.

However, Demi Moore's character renders a compelling argument and Cruise's character is convinced. The contest between him and the defense attorney—played by Kevin Bacon—becomes more than just a murder trial. The Marine Corps and indeed the entire military way of doing things—the Military Code—is on trial. As it turns out, the true antagonist in the film is the powerful and autocratic Marine commander played by Jack Nicholson. By far, the film's best scenes are the dynamic, emotion-charged confrontations between Nicholson and Cruise.

It was little wonder that, in February 1993, *A Few Good Men* was nominated for the Academy Award for Best Picture. Nicholson received a nomination for Best Supporting Actor, but the Best Actor Oscar nomination that Tom Cruise deserved was not forthcoming. However, we recognize that it was early in this great actor's career and it is certain that there will be other opportunities. Still a very young man at the time of *A Few Good Men*, Tom Cruise was indeed

Left: Tom Cruise in a scene still from his moving and thoughtful performance in *Far and Away*.

Below left: Tom Cruise with co-stars Demi Moore and Kevin Pollak in *A Few Good Men*.

Right: Tom Cruise in the white naval officer's uniform that he wore in his role as a US Navy attorney in *A Few Good Men*.

one of the top actors of the era. He had clearly evolved artistically beyond being just another member of the 'Brat Pack'—far beyond. To quote Paul Newman, 'Tom may be the only survivor' of the Brat Pack.

Cruise was never comfortable with the label, considering himself neither a brat nor part of a pack. He chose his roles judiciously, while the other so-called Brat Packers got stuck in *The Breakfast Club* mold, playing spoiled, aloof, somewhat troubled kids, and ended up becoming indistinguishable from each other. But the movie-going public of the 1990s wasn't in the mood for brooding. We wanted somebody to make us feel good. Cruise, with his infectious smile and optimistic attitude, was able to do that.

By the early 1990s, many of the most promising Brat Packers had faded away, and in their place, a new crop of young actors had appeared on the scene, among them Julia Roberts, Patrick Dempsey, Winona Ryder, Christian Slater, Kiefer Sutherland and Keanu Reeves. *Us* magazine dubbed them the Cruise Generation.

Having learned from that earlier wave's mistakes, this group followed the lead of Tom Cruise. They were an eager, twentysomething crowd and determined to make it where many of the Brat Pack had failed. Clearly, Tom Cruise had outdistanced the packs. He had become a shining star in Hollywood's firmament and was destined to join the ranks of Hollywood's most famous leading men.

INDEX

FILMOGRAPHY